Family Scrapbook

Home Life
in the 1930s and 40s

Faye Gardner with Joyce Williams

Evans

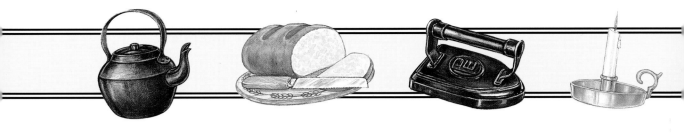

Published by in 2005 by Evans Brothers Limited
2A Portman Mansions
Chiltern St
London W1U 6NR

British Cataloguing in Publication Data
Gardner, Faye
Home Life in Grandma's Day
1.Farm Life – Wales – History – 20th century – Juvenile literature
2.Children – Wales -Social conditions – 20th century – Juvenile literature
3.Great Britain – Social life and customs – 20th century – Juvenile literature
4. Farm Life – Wales – History – 20th century – Juvenile literature
I. Title
II. Williams, Joyce
942.9

ISBN 0 237 53054 6
13 digit ISBN (from January 2007) 978 0 237 53054 9

Acknowledgements
Planning and production by Discovery Books Limited
Edited by Faye Gardner
Designed by Ian Winton
Commissioned photography by Alex Ramsay
Illustrations by Stuart Lafford

The publisher would like to thank Joyce Williams for her kind help in the preparation of this book.

For permission to reproduce copyright material, the author and publishers gratefully acknowledge the fol-
lowing: The Advertising Archive Limited: 24; the art archive: 15 (right); The Hulton Getty Picture
Collection Library: 14, 17 (top), 22-23 (top); Leominster Museum: cover (middle right), 8, 11, 16, 24 (bottom); The Board of Trustees of the National Museums and Galleries on Merseyside (Stewart Bale
Archive): 12-13 (centre); The National Museum of Wales: 9 (top), 12 (left), 20, 21 (top), 27 (bottom),
28; The Robert Opie Collection: Cover (left, top right), 13 (right), 15 (left), 17 (bottom), 18, 19, 22 (bottom), 23 (bottom) 25, 26, 27 (top) Rural History Centre, University of Reading: 10 (top); Shropshire
County Museum Service: 9 (bottom).

CONTENTS

'Life on our farm was hard.'

My name is Joyce and I am a grandmother. I have two grandchildren, Ellie, who is twelve, and Hannah, who is eight.

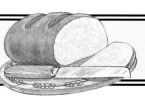

I was born in 1934, before the Second World War. When I was young, I lived on a farm near a small town called Knighton in Wales. The picture below shows you how the town looked then. My dad was a farmer and my mum was a housewife. I had a younger sister called Ruth to play with. Our grandparents lived on another farm nearby.

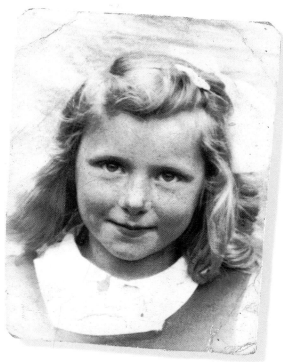

Life on our farm was hard. We didn't have tractors or machines to help us with the work. We were always very busy. I am going to tell you about our home and what life was like then.

 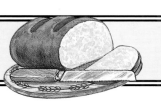  

'My sister and I helped on the farm.'

On our farm we kept sheep, pigs, cows and chickens. We grew **grain** and vegetable crops, too. We lived in a long-house, which was built out of stone.

The long-house was split into two parts: we lived in one half and in the winter the animals lived in the other.

My sister and I helped on the farm. Ruth milked the cows and I collected the eggs from the hens. At **harvest** time we helped pick the potatoes and swede. Every summer there was haymaking in the fields. We used long rakes and pitchforks to pile the loose hay into haystacks. The hay was used to feed the animals in the winter.

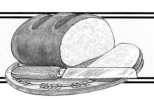

'We walked everywhere.'

We didn't have a car because they were too expensive. We walked everywhere, or went in a pony and trap like this one. Ruth and I had to walk five miles (8 km) to school and back every day. This is what our school looks like today.

Parish Church, Knighton

Before and after school, we had to help Mum in the house. We worked on Saturdays too, but had a day off on Sundays. We were still busy though, because we had to go to church in Knighton three times! In the evening Mum and Dad took us in the pony and trap, but the other two times we had to walk. That meant we walked twelve miles (19 km) altogether. I was very fit when I was young!

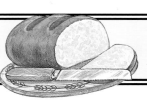

'An evacuee came to live with us.'

During the war, an **evacuee** called Jack came to live with us. He was from Liverpool. His parents sent him to the countryside because the city was being badly bombed. This is how Liverpool looked then.

Jack liked to play with the lambs on our farm.

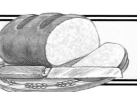

The war forced many men to leave their families to fight in the **armed forces**. My dad stayed at home because he was a farmer. Farmers were needed to grow food for the rest of the country to eat.

A lot of jobs on the farms were done by women who worked for the **Women's Land Army**. Two women called Gwynne and Mary came to work on our farm.

For a healthy, happy job

Join the
WOMEN'S
LAND
ARMY

For details:
APPLY TO NEAREST W.L.A. COUNTY OFFICE OR TO W.L.A. HEADQUARTERS 6 CHESHAM PLACE LONDON S.W.1 STREET

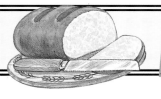

'We went to bed by candlelight.'

The house was cold in winter, because we didn't have central heating. I slept in the same bed as my sister to keep warm! Most of the rooms had an open fireplace in which we burned wood to heat the house.

The living room was my favourite place because it had a huge fireplace. It was the only room that was warm and cosy.

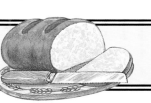

We lit paraffin heaters in the rooms that did not have a fireplace. The paraffin smelt horrible and made the walls very damp. Sometimes the wallpaper fell off!

There were no electric lights in our house. We used oil lamps in the evenings and went to bed by candle-light. My sister and I used to go upstairs together because it was so dark and spooky.

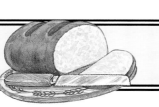

'We got our water from a pump outside.'

Our house did not have running water. We got our water from this pump outside.

My grandad used to get water from this pump, too.

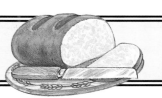

Most people did not have toilets or bathrooms inside their houses. We washed at the kitchen sink downstairs and had a bath in the kitchen, too!

Our toilet was in a shed at the bottom of the garden. It was not very nice. There were two holes in the ground and a little wooden seat to sit on. It was very cold in the winter! We used to cut up old newspapers into small squares for toilet paper.

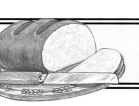

'Everything had to be washed by hand.'

Mum always did the washing on a Monday. There were no washing machines, so everything had to be washed by hand. We scrubbed the clothes on a **washboard** to get them clean.

THEN A NEIGHBOUR TOLD ME TO TRY FAIRY FOR ALL MY WASHING. IT'S WONDERFUL! MILD, BUT THOROUGH.

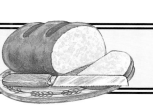

The clothes were squeezed through a mangle to get the water out. Then they were hung on a line outside, or in front of the fire to dry.

Ironing was hard work, too. We didn't have an electric iron. Instead we used flat irons, which were heated on top of a **range** in the kitchen.

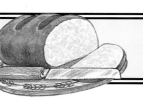

I ironed the clothes on a big blanket on top of the kitchen table. My arms used to ache because the irons were so heavy.

'The streets were full of stalls.'

Thursday was shopping day and my favourite day of the week. It was market day in Knighton and Dad took us there in the pony and trap. The streets were full of stalls selling fruit and vegetables.

ENGLISH COOKING APPLES 3P LB

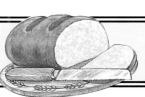

The farmers brought their animals to sell at the cattle market. Most of the farmers did not have lorries or vans. They had to walk the animals down the roads with their sheepdogs. There was always a lot of shouting and whistling!

Every September some of our sheep were sold at the market. I used to help Dad walk them to town. It was my job to run ahead and open the gates in the fields to let the sheep through.

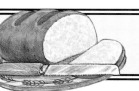

'Everyone was given a ration book.'

During the war there was not enough food in the shops and some things had to be **rationed**. We could only buy a certain amount of meat and other foods each week. People spent a lot of time queuing for food.

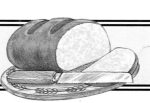

Everyone had a **ration book** which said how much food they could buy. The food rations in this picture would have to last one person for a whole week!

My family was lucky because we could get food from our farm. We always had plenty to eat. It was harder for people in cities to get fresh food.

The government encouraged families with gardens to grow their own vegetables. They put up posters like this one.

DIG FOR VICTORY

For their sake -
GROW YOUR OWN
VEGETABLES

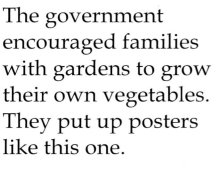

'The cooking was done on the kitchen range.'

Every Friday Mum made bread and cakes. The cooking was done on the kitchen range.

On one side of the range there was a **boiler** which heated our water, and on the other there was an oven for baking.

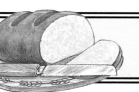

There was a fire in the middle of the range where we burned small logs to make it hot. We used the bellows you can see on the wall to make the fire burn up. We had to wait nearly two hours before the oven was hot enough to bake the bread.

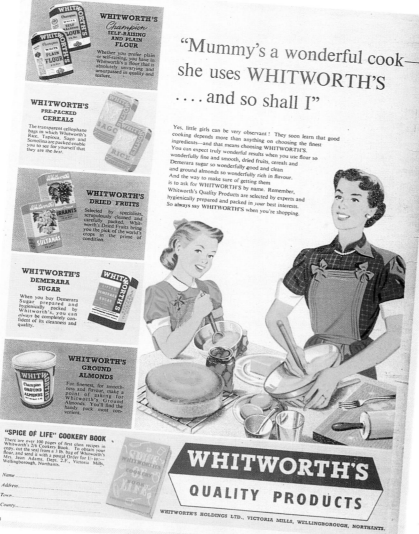

Sometimes Mum baked currant buns as a treat. The kitchen was always nice and warm on a Friday. It smelt good, too!

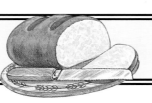

'We didn't have a fridge.'

We didn't have a fridge or freezer to keep the food in. We had a huge cupboard called a pantry. It was so big you could walk around inside. It had lots of wooden shelves to store the food on and the floor was made of stone to keep it cool.

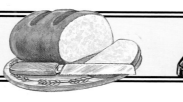

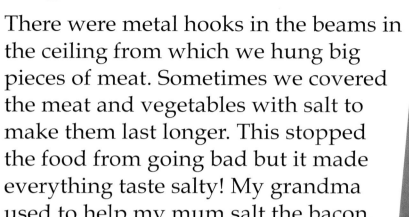

There were metal hooks in the beams in the ceiling from which we hung big pieces of meat. Sometimes we covered the meat and vegetables with salt to make them last longer. This stopped the food from going bad but it made everything taste salty! My grandma used to help my mum salt the bacon.

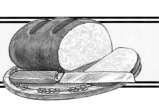

'We enjoyed ourselves.'

When I was young, we didn't have much spare time for hobbies or relaxing. We were too busy with the housework and farmwork.

But we enjoyed ourselves all the same.

GLOSSARY

Armed forces The army, navy and airforce.

Boiler A tank in which water is heated.

Grain A seed crop, like wheat or barley.

Evacuee Someone who was moved from a city made dangerous by bombing, to a safer place in the countryside.

Harvest The time of year when ripe crops are picked.

Range An oven heated by wood or coal.

Ration To limit the amount of something that people are allowed when it is in short supply.

Ration book A book of tickets used by people to buy rations.

Washboard A wooden or metal board with ridges that is used for scrubbing clothes.

Women's Land Army A force of young women who worked on farms to replace the men who had joined the armed forces.

OTHER BOOKS TO READ

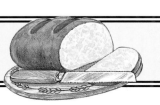

INDEX